THE TOILET BOOK

Gaming

by

Herman Cooper

ISBN: ISBN: 9798322352549

Contents

INTRODUCTION

Dear gamers,

Welcome to "The Toilet Book - Gaming" - your ultimate guide to the fascinating world of video games, designed for the most unusual but undeniably productive moments of the day. Yes, you read that right. This book is for those quiet moments when you need to retreat to the bathroom and have a little time to yourself.

Why a book about gaming for the bathroom? Well, because we believe that the passion for video games knows no boundaries - not even the bathroom door. Gaming is a universal language that connects us, stimulates our creativity and immerses us in worlds as rich and diverse as reality itself.

In this book, we take you on a journey through the pixel waters of gaming history, revealing curiosities that will surprise even the most die-hard fans and sharing anecdotes that show just how deep and influential our love of gaming really is. From its beginnings in pixelated 2D worlds to the breathtaking virtual realities of today, together we explore how video games have shaped art, culture and even the way we think and feel.

But "The Toilet Book - Gaming" is more than just a collection of facts and stories. It is a tribute to you - the gamers - who push the boundaries of what is possible every day and make the gaming community a place where everyone is welcome.

So make yourselves comfortable (we know where you are) and dive into the pages of this book. Laugh, learn and be inspired.

Have fun,

Herman Cooper

CHAPTER 1

PRESS START

- The first commercially successful video game was "Pong", a simple tennis game released by Atari in 1972.

- "Space Invaders" (1978) was so popular in Japan that it led to a shortage of 100-yen coins.

- The first video game ever programmed is called "Spacewar!". It was developed at MIT in 1962.

- Ralph Baer, who is considered the "father of video games", developed the first game console for home use, the "Magnavox Odyssey", in 1972.

- "Pac-Man" was originally released as "Puck Man" in Japan. The name was changed to avoid vandalism that could change the title to an inappropriate word.

- The inventor of "Tetris", Alexey Pajitnov, only received royalties in 1996, twelve years after the game was released, because he had developed the game in the Soviet Union.

- The characters in "Donkey Kong" were originally designed for a Popeye game, but the concept was changed due to licensing problems.

- "The Legend of Zelda" was one of the first games to use a battery to save game states.

- Atari buried thousands of copies of the flop game "E.T. the Extra-Terrestrial" in a landfill in New Mexico, which was just an urban legend for decades until the games were actually unearthed in 2014.

- The first gaming trade fair, the Consumer Electronics Show (CES), took place in 1972.

- The first Easter egg in a video game was hidden in "Adventure" for Atari. It showed the name of the developer, Warren Robinett.

- "Zork", one of the first text adventure games, was originally developed on a PDP-10 minicomputer at MIT.

- Nintendo began as a playing card company in 1889, long before they entered the video game industry.

- The highest score ever achieved in "Pac-Man" is 3,333,360 points and requires perfect play of 256 levels.

- Steve Russell, the creator of "Spacewar!", needed around 200 hours to program the game.

- "Pong" was not patented because the technology was not new; this allowed a flood of imitations.

- The first known "bug" in a computer program was actually a physical bug (a moth) found in the relays of a Mark II computer in 1947, which inspired the term "debugging".

- "Missile Command" was inspired by its inventor's fears of nuclear war.

- The inventor of "Super Mario" and "The Legend of Zelda", Shigeru Miyamoto, was not originally a programmer, but an industrial designer.

- "Asteroids" and "Lunar Lander" were two of the first games to use vector graphics, a technique that drew lines directly on the screen, as opposed to the raster-based graphics used in most earlier and later games.

- The first known video game tournament took place in 1972 at Stanford University for the game "Spacewar!". The main prize was a year's subscription to Rolling Stone magazine.

CHAPTER 2

ATARI

- Atari was founded in 1972 by Nolan Bushnell and Ted Dabney. The company is considered a pioneer in the video game industry.

- The name "Atari" comes from the Japanese board game Go and stands for a situation similar to checkmate in chess. Bushnell, a fan of Go, chose the name because he believed that Atari would dominate the video game industry.

- "Pong", Atari's first game, was originally designed as a training exercise for a new engineer and not planned as a commercial product.

- Atari played a key role in the emergence of the home console market with the launch of the Atari 2600 console in 1977, also known as the VCS (Video Computer System).

- "E.T. the Extra-Terrestrial" for the Atari 2600 is considered one of the worst video games of all time and is often blamed for the video game crash of 1983.

- Atari also released some of the first computer systems for home use, including the Atari 400 and Atari 800, both introduced in 1979.

- Despite its success in the early years of the video games industry, Atari suffered heavy financial losses, which led to the company being split up in 1984.

- Atari's famous logo, the "Fuji" symbol, is meant to represent a mountain and stands for strength and endurance.

- Atari also supported the development of the first successful arcade game "Computer Space", which was developed by Bushnell and Dabney before Atari was founded.

- The Atari 2600 was in production for almost 15 years, a testament to its popularity and influence.

- The Atari 5200, the successor to the 2600, was criticized for its unreliable non-centering joysticks and could not repeat the success of its predecessor.

- "Asteroids" and "Centipede" are two of Atari's best-known arcade games, which were later also released for the Atari consoles.

- In 1982, Atari sponsored the "Atari World Championships", one of the first nationwide video game competitions in the USA.

- Nolan Bushnell founded Chuck E. Cheese to showcase and monetize more arcade games from Atari.

- Atari tried to enter the home computer market in the 1980s but was unable to assert itself against competitors such as Apple and Commodore.

- The Atari Lynx, launched in 1989, was the first handheld games console with a color display, but was unable to compete with Nintendo's Game Boy.

- Despite the ups and downs, Atari remains a symbol of the early days of video games and has a loyal fan base that upholds the classic games and consoles.

CHAPTER 3

NINTENDO

- Nintendo was originally founded in 1889 by Fusajiro Yamauchi and began as a manufacturer of handmade hanafuda playing cards.

- The name Nintendo can be roughly translated as "let luck decide the sky".

- Before focusing on video games, Nintendo experimented with a variety of business models, including love hotels, a cab company and instant rice.

- The first video game developed by Nintendo was "EVR Race" in 1975, a horse racing simulation game.

- "Donkey Kong", one of the first games developed by Nintendo, played a key role in establishing Nintendo on the American market. The game was designed by Shigeru Miyamoto, who was later responsible for the creation of Mario and The Legend of Zelda.

- Mario, Nintendo's mascot, first appeared in "Donkey Kong" (1981) as a character called Jumpman.

- The Game Boy, which was released in 1989, is one of the best-selling consoles of all time. The included game "Tetris" contributed significantly to its success.

- The idea for "The Legend of Zelda" was inspired by Shigeru Miyamoto's childhood experiences exploring forests and caves near his home in Japan.

- Nintendo was originally against the release of "Pokémon" in the USA as they believed it would not be successful there. Pokémon became a worldwide phenomenon and is one of the best-selling video game series of all time.

- The Nintendo Entertainment System (NES) helped to revive the video games industry after the crash of 1983.

- Nintendo's strict quality seal, which can be seen on games and products, was introduced in response to the market crash of 1983 to reassure consumers that they were buying high quality products.

- "Super Mario Bros." was originally developed as a farewell to the NES, as Nintendo was already working on the next generation of consoles.

- Nintendo's first handheld games console was not the Game Boy, but the Game & Watch series, which was launched in 1980.

- "Luigi", Mario's brother, was first introduced in "Mario Bros." (1983) to enable two-player gameplay.

- Nintendo owns part of the Seattle Mariners MLB baseball team, although they sold a large portion of their shares in 2016.

- The Wii Sports game that came with the Wii console surpassed Super Mario Bros. as the best-selling video game of all time, thanks to the popularity of the Wii.

- The Wii Remote was born out of the desire to create a gaming device that anyone, regardless of age or gaming experience, could use intuitively.

- The idea for the Switch, Nintendo's console that can be used as both a portable and home system, came from observing how people use smartphones and tablets.

- Nintendo's headquarter in Kyoto, Japan, was originally a card production facility and later became the headquarters for their video game development.

- Shigeru Miyamoto, the creator of many of Nintendo's most famous franchises, including Mario, Donkey Kong and The Legend of Zelda, was heavily inspired by Walt Disney and originally wanted to become a manga artist.

CHAPTER 4

PLAYSTATION

- The original PlayStation was launched in Japan on December 3, 1994 and marked Sony's debut in the console market.

- The development of the PlayStation began as a joint project between Sony and Nintendo to develop a CD-ROM drive for the Super Nintendo, but the project fell through.

- The first game developed for the PlayStation was a racing game called "Ridge Racer", published by Namco.

- The PlayStation was one of the first games consoles to support 3D graphics in real time, which had a major impact on the development of video games.

- The PlayStation controller's characteristic four-button layout (triangle, circle, X, square) was designed to represent different functions: Triangle for camera angle, circle and X for yes/no decisions and square as a menu button.

- "Final Fantasy VII", one of the best-selling games on the PlayStation, helped popularize the genre of role-playing games (RPGs) in the Western world.

- The PlayStation 2, released in 2000, is the best-selling console of all time with over 155 million units sold worldwide.

- The PS2 was so popular that it was produced until 2013, even after the launch of the PS3 in 2006.

- The PlayStation 2 was backwards compatible, which meant that it could play games from the original PlayStation.

- Sony's decision to equip the PlayStation 3 with a Blu-ray drive contributed significantly to the victory of the Blu-ray format over HD DVD in the format war.

- The network for the PlayStation, PlayStation Network (PSN), was launched in 2006 and offered online gaming and the download of games and movies.

- The PlayStation 3 had a difficult start with high prices and a lack of exclusive games but recovered over its lifetime with price cuts and strong titles.

- "Gran Turismo", the PlayStation's best-selling franchise, has sold more than 80 million copies worldwide.

- The PlayStation 4 was released in North America on November 15, 2013, and sold over one million units in just 24 hours.

- The PlayStation VR, a virtual reality headset for the PS4, was launched in 2016 and brought VR gaming into the mainstream.

- The idea for the PlayStation's achievement system, known as 'Trophies', was inspired by similar systems on Xbox and other platforms and was first introduced in 2008.

- The iconic boot sequence and logo of the original PlayStation were designed by Takafumi Fujisawa, who wanted players to feel emotionally moved when they switched on the console.

- The PlayStation 3 offered the option to install an alternative operating system on release, which made the console popular with hackers and for some academic research projects. However, this feature was later removed by a firmware update.

- Sony has filed a patent for an AI assistant that could help players through difficult parts of a game by offering suggestions or help directly through the console.

- The PS5 was sold out almost everywhere shortly after its release, partly due to the global pandemic, which affected both production and supply chains, but also due to the huge demand.

CHAPTER 5

XBOX

- The first Xbox was launched by Microsoft in North America on November 15, 2001, marking Microsoft's first step into the console market.

- The development of the original Xbox was referred to internally at Microsoft as "Project Midway", a reference to the Battle of Midway, a turning point in the Pacific War during the Second World War, underlining Microsoft's ambition to conquer the console market.

- The name "Xbox" is originally derived from "DirectX Box", a reference to Microsoft's graphics API, DirectX, which is used for games on Windows PCs.

- Bill Gates, the co-founder of Microsoft, unveiled the Xbox together with wrestler The Rock (Dwayne Johnson) at the Consumer Electronics Show (CES) in 2001.

- The Xbox was the first console to offer a built-in hard disk for storing games and content.

- Xbox Live, the Xbox online service, was launched one year after the console release in November 2002 and revolutionized online gaming on consoles.

- The first game to support Xbox Live was "Phantasy Star Online", although "Halo 2" is often credited as the game that popularized the online service.

- "Halo: Combat Evolved", which was released at the launch of the Xbox, played a decisive role in the console's success, and became one of it´s best-selling titles.

- Microsoft had to pay a fine of 250 million US dollars to Nvidia to end production of the first Xbox earlier than planned due to disagreements over the price of the graphics chips supplied by Nvidia.

- The Xbox 360's "Red Ring of Death" bug led to one of the most expensive recalls in electronics history, with Microsoft spending over $1 billion on repairs and extended warranties.

- The Xbox 360 had a secret easter egg that remained undiscovered for more than a decade: If you open the system and examine the disk in Windows Explorer, you will find a small file with the name of the Xbox dashboard team.

- The Xbox 360 introduced "Achievements" that reward players for reaching specific goals in games, a concept that was quickly adopted by other platforms.

- Kinect for Xbox 360, a motion control system that does not require controllers, was launched in November 2010 and set a Guinness World Record as the fastest selling consumer electronics device.

- The Xbox One was originally able to recognize voice commands via Kinect, which led to some unwanted purchases when commercials that said "Buy Xbox" activated the console.

- Microsoft once ran an advertising campaign where they parked a real tank outside a PlayStation event to promote the Xbox.

- The Xbox One, the third generation, was released in November 2013 and was initially criticized for its high pricing and initial focus on TV functionality and DRM measures.

- "Project Scorpio" was the codename of the Xbox One X, the most powerful version of the Xbox One, designed specifically for 4K gaming and improved performance.

- The "Xbox Game Pass", launched in June 2017, is a subscription service that gives users access to an extensive library of games and is often referred to as the "Netflix for video games".

- Microsoft bought Mojang, the studio behind "Minecraft", in 2014 for 2.5 billion US dollars, making "Minecraft" an important title in the Xbox ecosystem.

- The Xbox community has supported several charitable initiatives over the years, including Gamers Outreach, an organization that delivers game consoles and games to children's hospitals.

- Phil Spencer, the head of Xbox, hid a real console in the background of his home office webcam footage during several livestreams before the official announcement of the Xbox Series S, showing how Xbox likes to play with its community.

CHAPTER 6

JRPGS

- JRPG stands for "Japanese Role-Playing Game". It refers to a video game genre that originated in Japan and is characterized by certain features, such as in-depth narratives, complex character development and often turn-based combat systems.

- The first JRPGs were heavily inspired by western RPGs such as "Dungeons & Dragons", but quickly developed their own identity and narrative style.

- "Dragon Quest", released in 1986, is considered the first true JRPG and set many standards for the genre, including the turn-based combat system.

- "Final Fantasy" was so named because the development team thought it would be their last game before the company went bankrupt - instead, it became their biggest success.

- Originally launched as a small game for the Game Boy, Pokémon has become one of the most successful multimedia franchises in the world.

- In Japan, "Dragon Quest" is so popular that there is an urban legend that schools and businesses remain empty on the day new games are released.

- "EarthBound" achieved cult status in the West, although it was only moderately successful in Japan.

- Golden game modules were produced for the release of "Dragon Quest III", which was intended to boost sales.

- JRPG soundtracks, composed by musicians such as Nobuo Uematsu and Koichi

Sugiyama, are performed in concert halls around the world.

- "Final Fantasy IV" introduced the Active Time Battle (ATB) system, which integrated real-time elements into the turn-based battles.

- Translation errors in JRPGs have led to numerous memes, including the infamous "All your base are belong to us" from Zero Wing.

- The "Persona" series is known for combining traditional JRPG elements with simulations of everyday life and psychological themes.

- The "Tales of" series is known for its combat system, which integrates real-time action into the battles of JRPGs.

- "Chrono Trigger" offers more than a dozen different endings.

- The "SaGa" series, known for its open world and non-linear narrative, began as a project that was originally planned as a sequel to "Final Fantasy".

- "NieR: Automata" combines JRPG elements with philosophical questions and a story that explores existentialism and human nature.

- JRPGs are known for often taking dozens to hundreds of hours to complete, making them a long-term endeavor for players.

- In Japan, there is a strong culture of "dōjin" or indie games, including JRPGs, which are often sold at fan conventions such as Comiket.

- "Final Fantasy VII" was one of the first JRPGs to offer a comprehensive 3D world and contributed significantly to the popularization of the genre outside Japan.

- Many JRPGs contain "Easter eggs" and hidden references to other games and media, which leads to a deep cultural interconnectedness within the genre.

- The soundtrack to "Final Fantasy VI" was one of the first video game albums to receive gold status in Japan.

- The "Shin Megami Tensei" series, launched in 1987, is one of the oldest running JRPG franchises and is known for its dark themes and complex stories.

- "Ni no Kuni: Wrath of the White Witch" was developed in collaboration with Studio Ghibli and is known for its breathtaking animations and soundtrack composed by

Joe Hisaishi, representing a rare collaboration between a video game developer and a famous animation studio.

- JRPGs have had a significant impact on global gaming culture by introducing themes and narrative styles from Japanese history and mythology to international gamers.

CHAPTER 7

BEAT'EM UP

- The term "beat 'em up" describes video games where the main objective is to defeat a variety of opponents through hand-to-hand combat, and is simply derived from the direct action of "beating" the opponents.

- The first game that is generally recognized as a beat 'em up is "Kung-Fu Master" from 1984, which was inspired by the adventures of Bruce Lee in the film "Game of Death".

- "Double Dragon", released in 1987, is considered one of the most influential games in the beat 'em up genre and introduced many elements that became standards of the genre, such as cooperative gameplay.

- The "Streets of Rage" series is famous for its music, composed by Yuzo Koshiro, which is considered groundbreaking for the use of electronic music in video games.

- "Final Fight", developed by Capcom, was originally intended to be a sequel to "Street Fighter", but developed into a game in its own right and had a significant impact on the genre.

- "Teenage Mutant Ninja Turtles: Turtles in Time" is one of the most popular beat 'em ups.

- Beat 'em ups were particularly popular in the late 80s and early 90s, when arcade games played a major role in gaming culture.

- Many beat 'em ups feature "combo" attacks, which allow players to perform more powerful attacks through a specific sequence of button inputs.

- Some beat 'em ups, such as "River City Ransom", integrate RPG elements by allowing character upgrades and customization.

- "Golden Axe" is known for its fantasy elements and the ability to ride mythical creatures, which offered a change of pace from the urban environments of many other games in the genre.

- The beat 'em up games in the "Dungeons & Dragons" series, such as "Shadow over Mystara", combine the genre with elements of classic role-playing games and offer a selection of characters with different abilities.

- In the 2000s, the popularity of beat 'em ups declined as interest in 3D games and other genres grew, but the genre is experiencing a renaissance thanks to indie developments and reissues of classic titles.

- "Scott Pilgrim vs. the World: The Game", based on the comic book series and movie, was praised for its faithful beat 'em up gameplay and homage to the genre.

- Beat 'em up games often have a very exaggerated depiction of violence, which in some cases has led to controversy and discussions about the depiction of violence in video games.

- "Battletoads", known for its high level of difficulty, is an iconic beat 'em up that is often cited as one of the hardest games of all time.

- Many beat 'em ups, especially arcade games, were known for being extremely challenging to encourage players to put in more coins to keep playing.

- "Cadillacs and Dinosaurs", based on the comic series "Xenozoic Tales", is a unique beat 'em up set in a post-apocalyptic world with dinosaurs.

- In Japan, beat 'em ups are often referred to as "belt scroll" games, a reference to how the game environment often moves horizontally like a conveyor belt.

- The social experience of playing beat 'em ups in arcades, often shoulder to shoulder with friends or strangers, contributed to the formation of communities and long-lasting friendships.

CHAPTER 8

FIGHTING GAMES

- "Street Fighter II" (1991) by Capcom revolutionized the genre by introducing the competitive multiplayer element and offering a variety of playable characters with unique moves.

- The first known game to be considered a fighting game is "Heavyweight Champ" by Sega, which was released back in 1976, but it was "Karate Champ" from 1984 that popularized the genre.

- In 1993, "Virtua Fighter" by Sega was the first fighting game to be realized entirely in 3D and influenced many subsequent 3D fighting games.

- "Killer Instinct" introduced the "Combo Breaker" system, which allows players to break out of long combo attacks by the opponent.

- "Dead or Alive" gained attention (and criticism) for its portrayal of female characters and the "bouncing breast" physics system.

- "Mortal Kombat" was actually born out of an attempt to develop a video game with Jean-Claude Van Damme as the main character, which ultimately did not work out, but led to the creation of this iconic fighting game.

- The Street Fighter II machines were often the scene of real physical confrontations when emotions boiled over between players, forcing arcade owners to take extra security measures.

- "Eddy Gordo" from "Tekken" was introduced in part because the developers wanted to create a beginner-friendly character whose random button mashing looks effective and spectacular.

- The blood and finishing moves in "Mortal Kombat" led directly to the founding of the ESRB (Entertainment Software Rating Board), which rates video games based on their content.

- The Evolution Championship Series (Evo) tournament began in a small ballroom in California and grew into the world's largest fighting game event.

- The character "M. Bison" from "Street Fighter" had to be renamed in the western version of the game to avoid legal problems with the boxer Mike Tyson (his Japanese name "M. Bison" became "Balrog" in the western version. In the Japanese version, "M. Bison" is called

"Vega" and the Western "Vega" is called "Balrog")

- "Guilty Gear Xrd" used a special technique to make 3D models look as if they were hand-drawn 2D animations.

- "Mortal Kombat" originally had the working title "Kumite", which was later changed.

- The famous "Hadouken" move in "Street Fighter" was inspired by an energy ball from the anime series "Dragon Ball".

- "SoulCalibur" used real historical weapons and fighting styles as inspiration.

- The "Fatalities" in "Mortal Kombat" were initially a secret feature that even some of the developers didn't know about.

- Some professional "Street Fighter" players use techniques such as "plinking" (priority linking) to increase the likelihood of successfully executing extremely difficult combinations.

- The complex background stories of many characters in fighting games have led to their own comic series, novels and even films.

- "Dead or Alive" introduced a "rock-paper-scissors" system for attacks, throws and blocks, which adds strategic depth to the gameplay.

CHAPTER 9

FIRST PERSON

SHOOTER

- The first known FPS game, "Maze War" (1973), was created on an Imlac PDS-1 computer at MIT and allowed players to move through a maze from a first-person perspective.

- "Doom" (1993) was so popular that in the 90s it was claimed to be installed on more PCs than the Windows 95 operating system, prompting Microsoft to port the game for Windows 95 to increase its appeal as a gaming platform.

- The "Quake" series pioneered the introduction of fully 3D-rendered environments and characters in first-person shooters, as opposed to the 2.5D sprites (sprite = graphic object) of "Doom".

- "GoldenEye 007" for the Nintendo 64 was one of the first console FPS games to achieve critical and commercial success and showed that the genre was viable outside of the PC.

- The developers of "Halo" began work on the game as a real-time strategy game. It was only later in the development process that it became the genre-defining FPS we know today.

- "Counter-Strike" began as a mod for "Half-Life" and became one of the most influential first-person shooters in terms of competitive gaming and eSports.

- "Wolfenstein 3D" is often wrongly referred to as the first first-person shooter, although there were important predecessors. However, it was the game that helped the genre make its breakthrough.

- The depiction of blood in "Doom" and other early FPS games led to an ongoing debate about the depiction of violence in video games.

- The exclamations "Boom Headshot!" and "Leroy Jenkins" were introduced to internet culture through FPS games, the former originating from the FPS gaming community and the latter from "World of Warcraft" but often quoted in FPS contexts.

- "BioShock" set new standards for storytelling in FPS games with its in-depth plot and the unique atmosphere of the dystopian city of Rapture.

- "Battlefield 1942" allowed players not only to fight on foot, but also to control vehicles and airplanes, adding tactical and large-scale battles to the genre.

- "Far Cry" was one of the first games to combine an open world with FPS elements, offering players unprecedented freedom of play.

- The iconic "Gravity Gun" in "Half-Life 2" became one of the most memorable weapons in video games.

- "Crysis" became famous for its phrase "But can it run Crysis?", which emphasizes the game's extremely high demands on the PC hardware and serves as a benchmark for the performance of a system.

- The title "Half-Life" refers to the radioactive decay in which a substance decays in half its original amount.

- The famous cake in "Portal" was inspired by a cake bought by a developer from a nearby supermarket. The cake became a recurring joke within the development team before becoming a central element of the game.

- "Call of Duty" was referred to internally by the developers as "the Spielberg game", inspired by "Saving Private Ryan".

- "Quake" was one of the first games to introduce online multiplayer deathmatches and thus had a lasting impact on the first-person shooter genre.

CHAPTER 10

POINT

AND

CLICK

ADVENTURE

- The first point-and-click adventure game was "Mystery House" (1980), which was published by Sierra On-Line and was the first graphic adventure game ever.

- "Monkey Island" was partly inspired by the Disneyland attraction "Pirates of the Caribbean", resulting in one of the most iconic series in the genre.

- "Maniac Mansion" allowed players to choose from multiple characters, which dramatically changed the gameplay and walkthroughs - an innovation for the genre.

- The developers of "The Secret of Monkey Island" created the game so that it was impossible to die, which was a reaction to the frustration they felt with other games where players could easily die.

- In "Day of the Tentacle" there is a playable version of "Maniac Mansion" on a computer in the game, making it one of the first "games within a game".

- "Sam & Max Hit the Road" is based on a comic by Steve Purcell, which originally began as a side project while he was working at LucasArts.

- "Grim Fandango" was the first adventure game from LucasArts to be developed entirely in 3D and introduced the unique "GrimE" engine.

- The voice of the protagonist in "Broken Sword" was spoken by the same actor who also lent his voice to Bob in the French version of "Twin Peaks".

- "Myst", one of the best-selling PC games of all time, was developed by just two brothers.

- "Leisure Suit Larry" was one of the first games to introduce an age verification test to keep younger players out - a test that most could easily bypass.

- "Discworld Noir" was the first game to introduce dynamic weather in a point-and-click adventure.

- "The Dig" by LucasArts originally began as an idea for an episode of "Amazing Stories", a TV series by Steven Spielberg.

- "Beneath a Steel Sky" was one of the first games to be distributed completely free of charge as part of a magazine.

- "Phoenix Wright: Ace Attorney" combined elements of point-and-click adventure games with a courtroom drama simulation, creating a new sub-genre.

- "Hotel Dusk: Room 215" used the Nintendo DS by having to hold the device like a book.

- "Toonstruck" combined real filmed sequences with animated cartoons and starred Christopher Lloyd.

- In "Indiana Jones and the Fate of Atlantis" there were three different ways to complete the game, which was unusual for adventure games at the time.

- "Loom", developed by Brian Moriarty, was one of the first point-and-click adventure games to integrate music and sound into the puzzle design by requiring players to use music sequences to solve puzzles.

- At the end of the 1990s and beginning of the 2000s, the popularity of point-and-click adventure games declined as the market was dominated by action and 3D games.

Many studios that had specialized in the genre had to close or reorient themselves.

- The popularity of point-and-click adventure games experienced a renaissance in the 2010s thanks to digital distribution platforms such as Steam and mobile devices.

- Crowdfunding platforms played an important role in the revival of the genre by enabling the financing of projects such as "Broken Age".

CHAPTER 11

HORROR

- "Resident Evil" was originally conceived as a remake of Capcom's earlier game "Sweet Home", a horror RPG for the NES that was never released outside of Japan.

- The infamous "P.T." (Playable Teaser) for the canceled "Silent Hills" used the PlayStation 4 system clock to activate certain ghostly apparitions only at certain times.

- "Eternal Darkness: Sanity's Requiem" for the GameCube introduced a "Sanity" mechanic in which the character experiences hallucinations that can lead the player astray, including fake television messages.

- In "Fatal Frame" (also known as "Project Zero"), the plot is based on real Japanese urban legends and haunted places. The developers visited cursed places to gather inspiration for the game.

- "Silent Hill" used the fog not only as an atmospheric element, but also to circumvent the technical limitations of the PlayStation and not have to render too many polygons at the same time.

- "Amnesia: The Dark Descent" contains a hidden message from the developers that only appears if the player tries to modify the game with a cheat program.

- "Outlast" and its sequel were so intense that reports emerged of players fainting while playing.

- The design of "Pyramid Head" from "Silent Hill 2" is intended to represent the shape of an ancient method of execution, which should be seen as metaphorical for the protagonist's guilt.

- "Resident Evil 4" went through several development phases, including a version that deviated so drastically from the original concept that it was ultimately released as "Devil May Cry".

- In "Alien: Isolation", the alien AI was intentionally programmed to not know everything about the player's location to create a more realistic cat-and-mouse game.

- "Five Nights at Freddy's" was inspired by a failed family-friendly game from the developer in which the character movements were criticized as "creepy."

- "The Last of Us" was inspired by the real-life parasitic fungal infection "Ophiocordyceps unilateralis", which infects ants.

- "Until Dawn" uses the "butterfly effect" mechanic, in which the player's decisions can influence the course of the entire story, leading to dozens of possible endings.

- "SOMA" hides philosophical questions about consciousness and human identity in an underwater research laboratory full of horror elements.

- The creators of "Dead Space" were inspired by various horror films and books, in particular "Event Horizon" and "The Thing".

- "Layers of Fear" plays with the idea of schizophrenia by distorting the perception of the game world depending on how the player interacts.

- The horror elements in "Bloodborne" were inspired by H.P. Lovecraft's cosmic horror.

The game world and the creatures are clear allusions to his works.

- "Visage" was developed as a spiritual successor to "P.T." and uses a similar concept of a constantly changing house to create psychological horror.

- "Alan Wake" directly quotes works by Stephen King and mixes elements from his stories with Nordic myths.

CHAPTER 12

PLATFORMER

- The term "platformer" is derived from the platforms on which the game characters run, jump and climb to overcome obstacles and achieve goals.

- "Super Mario Bros." is considered to be the game that popularized the platform game genre and established many standards that can still be found everywhere today.

- The platform game genre has split into many sub-genres, including puzzle platformers, where the focus is on solving puzzles, and endless runners, where the aim is to get as far as possible.

- Some of the earliest video games were simple platform games. "Space Panic" (1980), although still without the ability to jump, is often considered one of the first games of this genre.

- "Castlevania" combined platform action with elements of adventure games and laid the foundation for the Metroidvania sub-genre.

- The success of platform games on mobile platforms has revitalized the genre, with "Super Mario Run" being a prominent example of the success of classic platformers in a new format.

- "Mirror's Edge" brought a fresh perspective to the genre by combining first-person platforming with a dystopian story.

- "Cuphead" is known for its challenging level of difficulty and its unique graphic style, which is reminiscent of American cartoons from the 1930s.

- "Shovel Knight" pays tribute to classic 8-bit platformers while integrating modern game design principles.

- The unexpected success of "Braid" (2008) helped to spark interest in indie platformers and showed that the genre still has plenty of room for creative storytelling.

- "The Floor is Lava", actually a children's game, was adapted as a video game.

- The introduction of co-op modes in platform games, such as in "New Super Mario Bros. Wii", has expanded the social gaming experience of the genre.

- "Super Mario Bros." (1985) sold over 40 million copies, making it the best-selling game of the 20th century.

- "Mega Man" was originally called "Rockman" in Japan, a reference to the music genre, which is also reflected in the names of many of the characters.

- "Crash Bandicoot" was known internally at Naughty Dog as "Sonic's Ass Game" because the camera was positioned behind the protagonist, unlike the side-scrolling Sonic games.

- "Prince of Persia" (1989) was one of the first games to use rotoscoped animations to create realistic character movements.

- "Super Mario 64" (1996) set new standards for 3D platform games and was one of the first "open world" games of the genre.

- "Sonic the Hedgehog" was developed as a mascot for Sega to compete with Nintendo's Mario.

- "Rayman" (1995) was originally developed for the Atari Jaguar console and is one of the few successful titles released for the system.

- "Psychonauts" was praised for its story and humor, but initially had poor sales figures until it finally achieved cult status.

- "Kirby" was named after the lawyer John Kirby, who defended Nintendo in a copyright dispute with Universal Studios.

- "Celeste" was developed as a game exploring anxiety and depression and received recognition for its sensitive treatment of these issues.

- "LittleBigPlanet" offered players extensive tools to create their own levels, which led to a huge online community of level designers.

CHAPTER 13

STRATEGY

- "Dune II" is generally regarded as the first modern real-time strategy (RTS) game and laid the foundation for many concepts that were standardized in later RTS games.

- The "Civilization" series was inspired by a book called "The Rise and Fall of the Third Reich" and the board game "Risk". Sid Meier wanted to create a game that encompassed all of human history.

- "StarCraft" is so popular in the South Korean eSports scene that the game has its own TV channels and professional leagues.

- "Age of Empires II" is so popular that it is still receiving new expansions more than two decades after its initial release in 1999.

- In "Command & Conquer: Red Alert", a game mode was originally planned that would have allowed the use of a "time machine", but it was removed from the game before release.

- "Total Annihilation" was one of the first strategy games to use 3D graphics and introduce a realistic physics engine for projectiles.

- "Warcraft: Orcs & Humans" was originally conceived as a game in the "Warhammer" universe, but Blizzard couldn't reach a licensing agreement, so they developed their own universe.

- "SimCity" was born out of creator Will Wright's interest in creating cities within the game "Raid on Bungeling Bay".

- "League of Legends", a game that emerged from the RTS genre, was originally developed as a "Defense of the Ancients" (DotA) mod for "Warcraft III".

- "Company of Heroes" offered one of the first cover systems in an RTS that incorporated the landscape and destructible environments into the strategy.

- "The Settlers" was originally based on a never-published board game developed by its creator Volker Wertich.

- "Homeworld", the first fully three-dimensional RTS, let players fight battles in all three spatial dimensions.

CHAPTER 14

ACTION

ADVENTURE

- "Tomb Raider" was originally conceived with a male protagonist before the developers opted for Lara Croft, one of the first female video game heroines.

- "Metroid" only reveals at the end that the main character Samus Aran is a woman, which was a big surprise at the time.

- "Assassin's Creed" originated from ideas for a "Prince of Persia" spin-off, but developed into its own franchise with a unique historical setting.

- "Uncharted: Drake's Fortune" began as a fantasy game before Naughty Dog decided on a modern adventure.

- "Okami", known for its ornate graphics based on traditional Japanese ink painting, was one of the last major games to be released for the PlayStation 2.

- "God of War" (2018) integrated a single, uninterrupted camera shot for the entire game, a technical masterpiece.

- "The Witcher 3: Wild Hunt" contains over 450,000 words of dialog, more than twice as much as an average novel.

- "Red Dead Redemption 2" developed its own weather system that realistically simulates local weather events such as storms and fog.

- The idea for "Horizon Zero Dawn" came from an internal competition at Guerrilla Games, in which employees were able to suggest new game concepts.

- "Beyond Good & Evil" was inspired by the works of photographer Henri Cartier-Bresson, in particular the way he tells stories through images.

- "BioShock" is set in the fictional underwater city of Rapture, which was conceived as a utopian society before it drifted into madness, based on the philosophical ideas of Ayn Rand.

- "L.A. Noire" used a revolutionary motion capture technique called MotionScan to capture the characters' facial animations to create realistic interrogation scenes.

- "Middle-earth: Shadow of Mordor" introduced the "Nemesis" system, which creates individual enmities and rivalries between the player and certain NPCs.

- "A Plague Tale: Innocence" combines historical events with supernatural elements to tell a gripping story during the time of the Black Plague in France.

- In "Uncharted 2: Among Thieves" there is a scene in which Drake asks a Tibetan villager for directions and is completely ignored. This was actually a bug in the game that the developers found so entertaining that they left it in the game.

CHAPTER 15

RACING

- "Pole Position" (1982) was one of the first racing games with a 3D perspective and realistic racetracks.

- "Gran Turismo" was developed by Kazunori Yamauchi and his team, who were so detail-oriented that they took over 1,000 photos of each car to make them as realistic as possible in the game.

- "Need for Speed: Most Wanted" includes a hidden Easter Egg where players can find a giant donut that, when driven through, triggers a rain of tire parts.

- "F-Zero", released for the Super Nintendo, was one of the first games to use "Mode 7" graphics technology to create an illusion of depth and speed.

- "Wipeout" was so popular that it not only remained a game, but also inspired soundtracks, its own card game and even a TV series.

- "Ridge Racer" was one of the first games to include a CD with the game's soundtrack, which was a novelty at the time.

- "Sega Rally Championship" was one of the first games to introduce different driving surfaces and their effects on the driving physics.

- "Gran Turismo" has its own academy (GT Academy), which has existed since 2008. This partnership between Nissan and PlayStation enables the best players to launch real racing careers.

- "Dirt Rally" used real co-pilot recordings to make the game as realistic as possible. The recordings were made in real rally cars under racing conditions.

- "iRacing", an online racing simulator, is used by professional racing drivers for training and competition, especially during breaks in the real racing seasons.

- "Road Rash", the infamous motorcycle racing game, was one of the first games to combine violence and racing by allowing players to punch their opponents during the race.

- "Excitebike" for the NES was one of the first games to allow players to create their own tracks, a feature that was way ahead of its time.

- The original "Mario Kart" (Super Mario Kart for the SNES) was originally developed as a prototype called "Super Mario Kart R" and only featured Mario as a playable character.

- "Trials" began as a simple Flash game called "Trials Bike Pro" on a website called Miniclip before becoming a full-fledged game series for consoles and PC.

- "Snuggle Truck" was originally called "Smuggle Truck" and was intended as a satire on US immigration policy, in which players were supposed to drive immigrants across the border. Due to controversy, the game was changed to a more harmless version with cuddly toys.

CHAPTER 16

SPORTS GAMES

- For "Tony Hawk's Pro Skater", Tony Hawk originally received a cheque for 500,000 US dollars as an advance payment for his licensing rights - a sum that far exceeded his expectations and led him to lend his name to the game. Over time, this became one of the most lucrative decisions of his career.

- "Madden NFL" owes its name and part of its success to John Madden, the famous NFL coach and commentator. Madden insisted that the game must contain 11 players per team to ensure realism, a requirement that presented the developers with major challenges.

- The game "NBA Jam" contained hidden characters, including President Bill Clinton and Prince Charles, which was done without official approval and led to a series of discussions about the use of celebrities in video games.

- Konami's "Pro Evolution Soccer" (PES) series often struggled with licensing issues, which is why many teams and players appeared under fictitious names. This led to a lively community dedicated to creating and sharing mods to implement the real names and kits.

- "Fight Night Champion" was the first EA Sports game to be given an M (Mature) rating due to its realistic depiction of blood and violence in boxing.

- The developers of "SSX 3" worked closely with NASA scientists to simulate the dynamics of snow and its behavior in different environments, which set the game apart from other snowboarding games in terms of realism.

- "Virtua Tennis" was developed and published by SEGA and was one of the first games to license real tennis players with their specific playing styles and signature moves.

- The development team behind "Skate" used real skateboarders to advise and model the tricks and movements in the game, resulting in one of the most realistic skateboarding games.

- In "Madden NFL," there is often talk of the "Madden Curse," a superstition that says players who appear on the cover of the game will have a bad season or suffer injuries.

- "Wii Sports, bundled with the Nintendo Wii console, is one of the best-selling video games of all time and made video game tennis in the living room a global phenomenon.

- "Tony Hawk's Pro Skater" led to many players taking up skateboarding as a hobby. Tony Hawk himself said that the game had a huge impact on the popularity of skateboarding.

- "Mario & Sonic at the Olympic Games" united characters from Nintendo and SEGA in an official Olympic video game, a collaboration that would have been unthinkable in the beginning.

- The NBA 2K series from 2K Sports and the NBA Live series from EA Sports were direct competitors for a long time. However, NBA 2K managed to prevail, especially after NBA Live struggled with several dropouts and weaker ratings between 2010 and 2019.

- "Tony Hawk's Pro Skater 2" achieved an almost perfect score on Metacritic and is considered one of the best-rated video games of all time.

- The first known sports game is "Tennis for Two", which was developed by William Higinbotham at Brookhaven National Laboratory in 1958. It was played on an oscilloscope and is considered one of the very first video games.

CHAPTER 17

(ACTION) RPGS

- The very first RPG, "Dungeons & Dragons", was published in 1974 as a tabletop game and laid the foundation for the entire genre, both for video games and for pen-and-paper games.

- "Diablo" was initially designed as a turn-based game before the decision was made to develop it in real time, which drastically changed the gaming experience.

- "Baldur's Gate" brought the Dungeons & Dragons rulebook into the digital world and had a significant influence on the development of western RPGs.

- There are over 17 million different weapon combinations in "Borderlands 2".

- "Secret of Mana" was originally developed for the SNES CD add-on, which was created in collaboration with Sony, but was converted to the SNES module format after the partnership fell through.

- "Skyrim" by Bethesda contains hidden references and Easter eggs ranging from "Game of Thrones" to Swedish pop songs.

- "Dark Souls" designer Hidetaka Miyazaki once said that his inspiration for the game world came partly from his childhood, when he tried to read Western fantasy books that he only partially understood.

- During the development of "Diablo", the team originally experimented with a claymation technique for the character animations before deciding on classic 2D graphics.

- "Monster Hunter: World" took influence from real-life ecosystems and animal behavior. The developers spent time studying nature documentaries to make the interactions of the creatures in the game as realistic as possible.

- "Kingdom Hearts" was born out of a chance encounter between a Square developer and a Disney representative in an elevator. The conversation led to the idea of uniting Disney characters in one game.

- "Undertale" was developed almost exclusively by one person, Toby Fox, who was also responsible for the music. The game was funded through his Kickstarter campaign and exceeded all expectations of its funding goals.

- Three of the most influential figures in the Japanese role-playing game scene worked together on the development of "Chrono Trigger": Hironobu Sakaguchi (Final Fantasy), Yuji Horii (Dragon Quest) and Akira Toriyama (Dragon Ball).

- The "Mass Effect" series featured one of the first attempts to tell a cohesive story across multiple games, with decisions that have an impact across the entire trilogy.

- It is difficult to determine what is considered the first "official" Soulslike game outside of FromSoftware titles, as many games were influenced by "Dark Souls". "Lords of the Fallen" (2014) was one of the first games to be explicitly marketed as Soulslike and featured similar gameplay mechanics and design principles.

CHAPTER 18

FAMOUS

FRANCHISES

- "Pokémon" is based on creator Satoshi Tajiri's childhood experience of collecting insects. The idea of catching monsters in Pokéballs was inspired by his idea of how insects live in small spaces.

- The first "Super Mario Bros." game was designed so that Mario wears a hat because the developers had difficulties animating his hair.

- "The Legend of Zelda" was named after Zelda Fitzgerald, the wife of the famous American writer F. Scott Fitzgerald, because Shigeru Miyamoto thought her name sounded significant.

- "Minecraft" was originally called "Cave Game" while it was in the development phase. The first version of the game was programmed in just six days.

- "Call of Duty" was initially rejected by Activision because it was feared that it would not be able to compete with the then dominant "Medal of Honor".

- "Tetris" was developed by a Soviet software engineer, Alexey Pajitnov. The name is derived from "Tetra", the Greek word for four, as each game piece consists of four squares.

- "Halo" was originally intended as a real-time strategy game for the Mac before it was turned into a first-person shooter for the Xbox.

- "The Elder Scrolls V: Skyrim" contains over 60,000 speaking lines. The recordings for this took over 3 years.

- "The Witcher 3: Wild Hunt" includes a quest inspired by an actual fan of the game who passed away during development.

- "World of Warcraft" is so extensive that players have collectively spent more than 6 million years in the game world.

- "Resident Evil" was released in Japan as "Biohazard". The name had to be changed because a trademark right for the name "Biohazard" already existed in the USA.

- The "Elder Scrolls" series was originally conceived as a gladiator game before it became one of the leading open role-playing franchises.

- "Grand Theft Auto" (GTA) was originally to be called "Race'n'Chase" and players were to have the option of playing cops or gangsters.

- In "Metal Gear Solid", players can simplify a boss fight by simply changing the date on the PlayStation console - waiting until the opponent dies of old age.

- "Half-Life" was originally called "Quiver", inspired by a military base in the novel "The Mist" by Stephen King.

- Sonic's original name was "Mr. Needlemouse". This name was used in the development phase before it was changed to Sonic.

- "Fortnite" was originally conceived as a co-op survival game. Epic Games added the battle royale mode, which led to the game's overwhelming success.

CHAPTER 19

STUDIOS &

DEVELOPERS

- Capcom's name is a portmanteau of "Capsule" and "Computers", a reference to its original business model of distributing software on cartridges (capsules).

- Before founding *Valve* and developing "Half-Life", Gabe Newell and Mike Harrington worked at Microsoft. They left the company to realize their vision of their own game.

- The founders of BioWare, Ray Muzyka and Greg Zeschuk, were originally doctors. However, they opted for the path of game development and created iconic series such as "Mass Effect" and "Dragon Age".

- "Grand Theft Auto" (GTA) was developed by DMA Design, which was later renamed Rockstar North.

- Naughty Dog, the studio behind "Crash Bandicoot", "Uncharted" and "The Last of

Us", began as a small garage project by Andy Gavin and Jason Rubin when they were still at school.

- "Minecraft" was originally developed by Markus Persson alone and later published by his company Mojang before being acquired by Microsoft for 2.5 billion dollars.

- FromSoftware, known for the "Dark Souls" series, started out as a software company that mainly worked on business apps before turning to game development.

- CD Projekt Red, the studio behind "The Witcher" and "Cyberpunk 2077", started out as a small company localizing games from the West for the Polish market.

- Blizzard Entertainment began under the name Silicon & Synapse and developed games such as "The Lost Vikings" before becoming one of the most influential studios in the industry.

- Tim Schafer, founder of Double Fine Productions and creator of "Psychonauts", began his career at LucasArts, where he worked on "Monkey Island".

- Hideo Kojima, the creator of "Metal Gear Solid", originally wanted to become a film director, which explains the style of his games.

- "Angry Birds" was developed by Rovio Entertainment after they had already published 51 other games. The success of "Angry Birds" saved the studio from financial ruin.

- Rockstar Games once rented an entire village in England for a "Red Dead Redemption" party, with western decorations and costumes.

- The original idea for "The Last of Us" came from Neil Druckmann's master's thesis at Carnegie Mellon University. Druckmann began his career at Naughty Dog as an intern before rising to co-author and eventually creative director of "The Last of Us". Today he is Vice President at Naughty Dog.

THANK YOU

Dear readers,

I would like to thank you from the bottom of my heart. Thank you for making "The Toilet Book - Gaming" your faithful companion in those moments when ... well, you know. But seriously, without you and your passion for video games, this book would just be a collection of pages. You bring the stories to life and the characters into motion.

You are the hero with the controller (or the mouse, we don't discriminate) in your hand. You show that gaming and its community are so much more than just a hobby. It's a passion that unites us, inspires us and shows us that a gamer's heart beats in each of us - whether on the loo or in front of the screen.

May your batteries always be full and your internet connection stable. Let's continue to celebrate the joy of gaming and discover new worlds.

Thank you very much!

Your Toilet Book-Team!

NOTE FROM THE

AUTHOR

During the compilation of this book, great care and passion has been taken to bring you the most fascinating and entertaining stories from the world of gaming. Despite every effort to be accurate, in a field as diverse and wide-ranging as gaming history, not all information may be 100% correct.

"The Toilet Book" is primarily designed as an entertainment book, not an academic reference book. Our aim is to entertain you and at the same time expand your knowledge of gaming in a light and amusing way.

However, we apologize for any errors. We welcome all feedback and are grateful for any suggestions that will help us to improve the content of future editions.

Enjoy reading and thank you for your trust in our book!

ALREADY AVAILABLE:

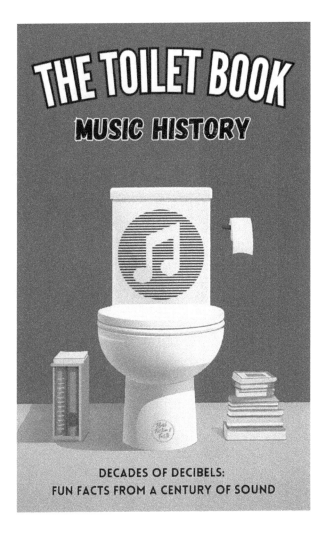

THE TOILET BOOK: MUSIC HISTORY

ISBN-13: **979-8860227620**

ALREADY AVAILABLE:

THE TOILET BOOK: MOVIE HISTORY

ISBN-13: **979-8861180429**

ISBN: ISBN: 9798322352549

www.ingramcontent.com/pod-product-compliance
Lightning Source LLC
La Vergne TN
LVHW092030060326
832903LV00058B/486